INTO
MOTHERHOOD

Jordan Moore

Dedication

My son, Dakota, thank you for making me a mama and showing me the true definition of unconditional love

My sister, Lizzy, thank you for being the mother and the friend I needed as I ventured on this journey and for all the years before

My husband, Cody, thank you for believing in me, showing me I am more than my past, and loving me despite it all

My best friend, Anam, thank you for the countless video calls and text messages throughout the day and into the early morning as we survived motherhood together

Contents

Preface   1

Parental Wounds   3

Building Life   33

In the Thick of It   47

Slightly Seasoned Mother   67

My Sweet Child   89

Divine Motherhood   105

Acknowledgements   127

Preface

I've been a self proclaimed poet for many years. Poetry became an outlet for me in the darkest of times. It gave me a way to describe the thoughts swirling around in my head in a more artistic way. Writing poetry allowed me to say what I needed without fear of being too forward or dark and giving voice to my beautiful, chaotic experience. As I ventured on the journey of motherhood, I found myself grasping for the sense of freedom that comes with pouring your honest thoughts out. So I started writing again. I wrote social media posts describing my time as a mother (included in this book) in hopes of finding solace in other mothers' experiences and giving that same solace to others. I received encouragement from family and friends to continue to share. Eventually, I found my way back to poetry. It sparked a new energy in me that I had been missing for a long time. I realized I didn't want to stop putting my words out in the world. Even if it only resonated with one person, it was worth it. I began writing more, collecting past poems, editing, and drafting them all to tell a story of how I grew *Into Motherhood*.

Parental Wounds

familial ties

held together by inconsequential knots

appearing to withstand wear and tear

further inspection shows fray

material is falling apart

time didn't treat it with kindness

knots are coming undone

now lie a mess

a pile of jumbled string

doors slam shut

voices carry

yelling slanders

quiet but serious fights behind closed doors

spankings and slaps brought to small children

abuse creates trauma

trauma that directs decisions in the future

a peanut

a small morsel of food

snatched from the cupboard

a child's thieving hands

consequence follows

a belt in the hand of her mother

the one meant to love and support

it moves in slow motion

until impact

bruises all along the body

when i was a young girl

a coward took my innocence

before he did so

he made me feel special

he loved me and i loved him

his intentions did little to prove

now he's with me wherever i go

his image haunts me

in a stranger's smile

when i make a mistake

or simply at home

his phantom voice echoes in my ears

telling me i'm not good enough

he's the only man for me

i'll never find love

i'm a useless, ugly hag

that will never make anything of herself

i feel his touch

in my dreams

and through the hands of another

he prowls in my head

on a good day

reminding me i'm not allowed

i don't want to believe him

but he manipulates thoughts

turning desires for family

into lost dreams

i thought the love from my father was beautiful

it made me feel good

special and worthwhile

often saving me from my mother's wrath

years later, the love morphed into something insidious

something creepily lurking around the corner

the love i was feeling

was grooming me all along

a single tear

glistens on her cheek

like a diamond in moonlight

it rests on her faded dimples

leaving a trail of moments lost:

the bedtime stories that never drifted her to sleep

the safety of a parental hug she never found

the wishes of birthday candles she never made

her mouth

sewn shut

by invisible threads

she lies there

silent

eyes locked on a single space

the tear finally breaks free

falling to the floor

shattering into a million more unforeseen moments

i grieve the loss of what could've been

i ache to hold the child

who grew up thinking she was worthless

believing she deserved punishment

i wish someone

somewhere along the way

could've saved us

i want it to end

the pain

the guilt

the memories

i want it to be erased

the hands on my skin

the lies uttered in my ears

the images of childhood

i want it to be taken

the thoughts

the false hope

the past

fragments of me remain frozen in time

unable to melt

i stay cold as i move forward

trying to wrap myself in the warm hope of the future

but my icy past won't let me

i'm frigid,

shaking,

remembering what's happened

an eternal winter in my mind

a reel of experiences

a movie screen in my head

painful, numbing pictures

blocking out reality

transporting me back

i close my eyes

i'm plagued with nightmares so vivid

i wake

taking time to accumulate to reality

it's always them

always

i feel

slaps from my mother's hand

my father's fingertips in my underwear

it's never that simple though

escalation is inevitable

their words cut deeper than anything

they slander me for my choices

gaslight me for speaking against the abuse

forbid me from living how i want

blame me for the family's pain

and convince me all the shit they throw at me is love

i don't want to go back

it hurts

i'm scared one day i'll wake up

my past will be the now

they'll be in control again

i'll be a walking corpse

merely surviving

i miss the home i never had

but i don't know why

when i was there, all i ever wanted to do was leave

the second i did, its siren call started

i returned only to be snared in her trap

one i would eventually escape

just for me to fall right back in

i listen to the same enticing song everyday

i don't want to go back

i don't want to return to the beautiful creature

because when i do, she reveals her true self

the one that sinks her teeth into the fleshy parts of me

just enough to hurt me but not enough to where others
        would believe

she sits back while i frantically search for help

no one listens

how could someone as beautiful as she do something so
        vile?

she laughs at me behind closed doors

acting just as confused as they do

she did nothing wrong

i'm creating my own monsters again

i've unknowingly built my life around it

keeping me stable and sane

without, my world crumbles

i need it to breathe, to function

it was taken from me

and ever since then

i've unconsciously chased after it

it is my protection

my skin

more a part of me than i care to admit

but understandably so

when it's taken

the rug beneath me is pulled

i'm lying on my back

staring straight up

with the wind knocked out of me

as i lie there

i try to accept the loss

but somehow, i always go back for it

control

i wish i was an armadillo

i would curl up and hide away

from the danger of this life

from undeserved happiness

from my dominating past

from the emotional puppeteer that

won't

let

go

but i can't hide

it's all very real and faces me everyday

i have to make a choice

to face it too

the pain ebbs and flows

a wave of remembrance crashes over me

bringing with it more pieces to the puzzle

it shows the faults in me

the mistakes i made

but these are only a few pieces in the bigger picture

it's not my fault for being a child that needed help

nor was i a burden for voicing my needs

and speaking against abuse

"there's always a light at the end of the tunnel"

it's too long and everything is dark

lost and dazed i trudge through the void

longing for a different path

myriad of memories cover the floor

rough despondent bricks

with sharp edges scrape my feet

making me collapse

i rise

become a paver

smooth triumphant stones

scattered among the brick

i can see the light

soles healing

exit over polished rock

sun is warm on my skin

i soak it in

before entering the next tunnel

i've come a long way

yet i feel far behind

barely making it past the start

while others cross the finish line

what is mental illness to me?

it's a label

major depressive disorder

generalized anxiety

attention-deficit/hyperactivity disorder

complex post-traumatic stress disorder

a storm looming overhead at all times

watching, waiting for the impending dark clouds to
        become turbulent

a lack of focus and headaches

throwing up because my body is overwhelmed with
        emotion

sitting on the bathroom floor, crying, hiding the shame

painting on a fake smile to mask the hurt

self sabotaging, flashbacks, destructive core beliefs

a perpetual cycle of being clueless as to when the tempest
        will rage and calling upon it myself

familiarity and twisted comfort

something to fall back on

self definition and expected perception

my downfall yet greatest strength

my ability to empathize

passion and understanding to help kids who suffer as well

self-awareness and insight

a capacity to find profound beauty and joy in the
        mundane

my greatest opportunity for growth

i've known her since i was six

she's been with me through every life event

when i lost my first pet

got my first report card

got on my first volleyball team

graduated high school

even when i met my husband

i wouldn't call her a friend though

in all those big moments

she sat next to me

distracting me with the "what ifs"

reminding me of past failures

sometimes she would rest

yet she always awoke

she stole my memories

placing them in a trophy case

full of crushed happiness

i trusted her

sometimes still do

she's always there

when i pull back

she cuts the rope

leaving me fumbling into one of her traps

i'm not sure i'll ever be able to defeat her

she agrees with me

saying she'll never stop trying to kill me

she's older now

she rests a lot more

i know she'll wake eventually

but i've learned to protect some hope

and she better be damned if she thinks

i'll let her take it

i've walked through life

with gum on my shoe

adding colorful wads

with every block

with a gunked up sole

i progressed slowly

between moments of sticking to pavement

i saw him approaching

scraper in hand

hope

wrenching my foot free

momentum sprang me into his arms

the future no longer quite so sticky

i felt like clutter growing up

an unwanted eyesore taking up space

i yearn for belonging

when i chose my husband and his family

i invested my energy

opened up

trusted

exposing myself almost immediately

get the inevitable abandonment out of the way

but it didn't

so i hung on

with a white knuckle grip

and from there

created my own home

Building Life

reminiscing

i see insecurity, fear, shame

a little girl so alone

watching, hoping for goodness

instead, she sees the injustices of the world

a metal spoon in the air—glistening in the light—

bracing herself for impact

words spit out of the mouth of those meant to love

cutting her down to nothing

hands of a trusted adult

reaching for her innocence and ripping it away

bullies who said they were friends and heartbreakers who
        said they cared

the little girl still exists somewhere inside of me

so i'm going to search for her

i'm going to hold her and love her

tell her what she needs to hear

"it won't always be like this"

tell her someday she'll have the power to walk away
        from it all

build a new life

be that adult for a child

she so desperately needed

an inner battle

am i ready?

will i ever be?

i want them now

i yearn to hold them

their fragile bodies

small fingers and toes

i yearn to kiss them

softly on their fuzzy heads

i yearn to watch them

grow

laugh

cry

sing

dance

to yearn for me

i want them now

but am i ready?

will i ever be?

my precious dream

dancing in my head

with a big smile

my precious dream

little bare feet running

on the hardwood floor

my precious dream

giggles ricochet

off picture filled walls

my precious dream

bedtime stories

daytime songs

my precious dream

snuggles to ease your fear

hugs just to love you

my precious dream

not yet alive

but oh so real

my baby

not yet born

but a part of me

a piece of my soul

i love them

with an incredible force

an image ingrained in my memory

one that hasn't occurred

yet, i remember

it feels so real

a mirage playing out in front of me

their minute bodies

chasing each other in a circle

heads tilted back with laughter in their bellies

a moment passes

they're there in my arms

my precious dreams

forever a piece of my soul

i gazed into the mirror of my upbringing

finding a strong desire to be better for my baby

fear told me the reflection was a looking glass into the
        future

i spoke to my round belly

manifesting the opposite to come to pass

vowing to change that course for us

shattering the glass

a picture in my mind

serenity among planned chaos

anticipation of my childhood dreams unfolding before
        my eyes

i've ached to be in this moment

never thinking i would

fear that once existed

now erased

the last year, my body tirelessly created life

nurturing, sustaining, feeding

building my beautiful baby boy

i'm so ready to meet him

soft music in the background calms me

smell of eucalyptus mint reminds me to take a
        breath

slowly, we begin

we, together, start his journey of departure

amongst the pain finding strength i didn't know i
        possessed

but would gladly take on just to have him in my arms

his father is near, guiding me

his presence anchoring me

i know with him, i am safe

with his soothing touch, i continue forward

i look into his eyes

i feel his love

love that created a miracle

starting us on this path of family

i've never felt so deeply for another than i have him

one final push

our baby is here

body so small yet so incredibly strong

two has become three

we sit in each other's arms

in awe of the beauty before us

this new person has poured into me

filling me with a love unimaginable

suddenly my dream has changed

i want to cultivate this blessing of mine

tend him with health, love, knowledge, compassion,
        empathy, strength

as we start this new life of ours

i'm humbled by the gift i've been given

i cry as i understand everything has changed

but smile because i wouldn't want it any other way

creating life is nothing short of a miracle

somehow my body found the way

to grow another set of organs and bones and skin

i tirelessly gave him my all just so he could exist

i watched myself instantly change

bad habits easily broken just for the mere idea he would
        be

i felt movement inside me

his tiny body shaping

longing since childhood grew stronger

i've wanted to be his mother since i was eight years old

daydreaming this life for myself

before understanding what it fully meant

days leading to his earth-side arrival

i was scared to face the reality

i, a flawed human being still figuring herself out,

would be given the most important role of mother

when labor started

pain came on suddenly and intensely

struggling to push through

eventually, together, we found our way into this new
beginning

he came into this world a little bundle of perfection

i looked at him

knowing nothing else mattered

In the Thick of It

I went to a mother's gathering soon after Dakota was born. While there we chose a word that resonated with us that we wanted to focus on for the remainder of the year. The word that stuck with me was "acceptance".
However, I've had a really hard time embracing it with all that has occurred since Dakotas earth side arrival. Since he was born, both Cody and I got laid off from our jobs, we've faced multiple illnesses, we've had 4 ER visits, one hospital stay, and dozens of appointments, all within a span of a few short months. The level of stress is beyond what I imagined bringing a child into this world would be like. As I sat reflecting my experience, I realized I forgot all about "acceptance".

Postpartum hit me like a freight train. All my symptoms are completely centered around Dakota and what I could be doing better for him. I've been focusing all my energy on what I'm doing wrong and how I'm failing my own son. My thoughts have been consumed by feelings of guilt, questioning my decisions, and running through an entire list of "what ifs". I've felt exhausted from the extensive process that taking care of a newborn is, let alone one with high medical attention needs. It's gotten so dark to the point I've even questioned my own validity of being his mother. I've told myself that Dakota would be better off with someone far more adequate than I. As I look at my child, I feel a level of love that's indescribable. I'm drawn to him in more ways than one. To watch this being that you built inside your own body, live a life outside of you is incredibly beautiful. I simply just want what's best for him. And I believe what's best for him is a mom who practices acceptance.

I accept that there are things outside of my control and I'm not to blame. All I can do is face what's comes at us and move forward with my best intentions.

I accept that there will be times that I do make mistakes. I will acknowledge them, apologize, and do better.

I accept that I cannot shelter my child from everything, even despite my best efforts.

I accept that I was made to be Dakota's mom and I AM the best woman for the job.

I accept that the choices we've made medically were made in efforts to help Dakota, even if they sucked in the moment.

I accept that time is a thief and I will no longer let it take mine by focusing on negativity.

I accept that there are times where I may slip up and still focus on negativity.

I accept that I do have help around me and I will utilize it.

I accept that my breastfeeding journey does not look how I thought or want it to but it is mine nonetheless.

I accept that this life is messy but I will try my best to make the most of it watching my son grow up with my husband by my side.

I love my little family more than anything. It's been a hard adjustment falling into this new role as parents. But I don't regret any of it. For Dakota, I would do it all over again, a million times.

– April 2024

Does anyone else absolutely loathe sleep regressions? I had heard about the 4 month sleep regression and tried to mentally prepare for it. Little did I know, 4 months is just a ballpark. It started for us a week after his 3 month anniversary. My sweet angel baby that smiles at everyone and everything and is calm and happy in any situation, will become a different person when it's nap time. He knows the routine. Light off, sleep sack, sound machine, try to feed, and in moms arms to be rocked to sleep. As soon as that transition to my arms happens, his body goes rigid, he screams, he thrashes his arms, he fights it with every fiber of his being. He will be calm, content, obviously tired, and then in an instant turn to the dark side. And it is SO HARD!!!! He has skipped naps, will wake up early from them still tired and refuse to go back down, and wake up as soon as he is put down in the bassinet (it's a lot of contact napping these days).

Something about this regression has not only flipped the switch in my calm babys mind but mine too. I don't consider myself an angry person. In fact, it's an emotion that has been super triggering for me in the past. So when I started to feel a deep guttural rage, I was taken aback and didn't know how to handle it. It started at the tips of my toes, all the way to my head. Everything in my body felt tense. There was a thick knot in my chest and throat. The term "blood boiling" finally made sense. Hearing his scream so close to my ear and his body fight mine as I tried to calm him caused a shift in my emotions. I was so overstimulated, exhausted, and frustrated with the "routine" of fighting sleep over and over again.

I don't quite understand fully how my emotions became so big so quickly but all I wanted to do was throw him in that moment. I just wanted him to stop, to fall asleep, and for me to not be in the position I was in. Let me clarify, I would never hurt my baby nor did I. But the intense feelings were there and it was like they came out of nowhere. Once he was finally asleep, I left the room and confessed (more like angrily expressed as I was still in the midst of it) my experience to Cody. I had never felt this way before and it lingered longer than I wanted.

As soon as the rage passed, I cried. I felt extreme guilt that those thoughts even entered my brain. I felt shocked that I could experience that emotion to that degree, let alone towards my child. I felt triggered, thinking of my own past and trauma. I felt confused as to why I had felt that way to begin with. I overall felt deeply disappointed in myself. I worked together with my therapist on where the feelings may have started and I came to the conclusion it was rooted in feeling like I was a bad mom to begin with. I was hurt that I could no longer easily get my baby to sleep or comfort him quickly in those moments. My mind told me that since I couldn't calm him down, I was a bad mother. And then it started a weird jumble of emotions that somehow leaped over to rage. It hurts to watch your child struggle and not be able to help despite your best efforts.

Since that rage filled moment, I've tried to put things into perspective. The regression is (hopefully) a short period of time. It is also a time indicating a huge jump in development. While it is still hard, the regression doesn't reflect my job as a parent, it just simply is. Even though it's difficult to get all the things done right now with contact naps, someday he's not going to want to snuggle me all the time so enjoy it while I can. And at the end of the day, I controlled my anger and didn't let it consume me. I allowed myself to feel what I needed to and processed all the gunk.

Rage is a scary feeling and it's less talked about than PPD. I think it's because there's a fear if we admit what's going on, people are going to judge and take our babies away. So I'm here to say, the rage is real, it's scary and hard, but that doesn't make you a bad mom. If anything, it makes you a good one for recognizing those feelings and not acting on them.

    — April 2024

As an individual with ADHD, getting things done is a process. I will start one task and get distracted with another one and in the middle of doing that task, get distracted with another and so on. I've learned to try and embrace it. The more I fight it and tell myself it's something bad, surprisingly, the less productive I am. When I allow myself to just move from one task to the other (even if they are halfway done), I feel more focused and motivated. I know that sounds silly because the act of doing that is kind of the opposite. But for me, all the jumbled thoughts and actions make sense. So when I try to stop it or talk negatively to myself, it breaks my train of thought. I have learned that lists are my friend. I have lists on my phone, on whiteboards, on scraps of paper, on the fridge, and probably on Cody's phone too. When I write things down, the chaos in my head calms a little bit. It can help me avoid task paralysis. However, since being a mom, the chaos is more than usual. The distractions are more often and my "zen flow" is interrupted. I will start something as usual, but then Dakota spit up or needs a diaper change or he's crying or he woke up from his nap, etc. My to-do list takes longer to complete and chores get abandoned more often than I care to admit. It leaves me little time for myself and my hobbies. Showers get stretched out to every four days or so when I just can't stand the smell of my own body odor, most days I forget to brush my teeth and put on deodorant, I rarely wear "normal" clothes, I struggle to find time to eat, and I rarely (if ever) practice my hobbies. The swirling thoughts and never-ending to-do lists inhibit my ability to do self-care. I tell myself I can put those things off so that Dakota gets the attention he needs and so Cody can come home to a somewhat clean house and home-cooked meal.

It's so much easier to put off my own needs in knowing that by doing so, my family gets theirs met. However, I know this isn't sustainable. If I were speaking to a friend, I would tell them how important it is to take time for themselves, to embrace their hobbies, to get food in their belly, and to take a break. But how do you actually do that? There doesn't feel like enough time in the day to get everything done and take care of the family AND take care of myself. I hate the saying "you can't fill from an empty cup" because as a mom, I feel like I do that everyday. But when I look at the big picture, I want Dakota to know it's ok to put himself first sometimes. Sacrifice is beautiful and important but as most things, there's a balance. I don't want him to feel like he always has to sacrifice his happiness and wants for the happiness of others.

— April 2024

Cody's sister got married recently which meant family was in town. A lot of family that would meet Dakota for the first time. It was both exciting and nerve-wracking for me. As family members held him and played with him, my heart was overjoyed while also beating fast from anxiety. My internal dialogue was full of concern for my child and criticism of how others should be around him. "You're not holding him properly", "if you're gonna hold him, interact with him", "you should play with him like this so he's receiving the proper developmental enrichment", "we haven't done our OT exercises yet, I need to do them NOW". I didn't verbalize any of it but it was an almost constant barrage in my mind.

A few days later, I went to complete a task while Cody watched Dakota. When I came back, I asked varying questions related to what occurred while I was gone. "Did you do tummy time? How long did you play with him? Were you just on your phone the whole time? Etc" This isn't the first time I've hounded Cody with these questions and unfortunately it probably won't be the last. My sweet, patient husband took a deep breath, answered my questions, and moved forward. Later on, he told me that I wasn't allowing Dakota to be a baby. I was hurt and confused so I asked for clarification. He explained that I'm so focused on the next milestone and Dakotas development, I'm not leaving room for him to just exist. I was deeply offended and basically just scoffed at him.

As I allowed myself to reflect, I realized how accurate he was and how unaware of it I had become. I recalled the weekend at the wedding where my thoughts were so centered around just that. I hadn't allowed myself to relax and enjoy being around family to the fullest because I was so consumed about his safety, growth, and health. Now, don't get me wrong, it is still important to give your child enrichment and help them to achieve the next milestone. But I had become so obsessed with it, that it was practically my every thought. I found myself stuck in a logical fallacy loop. "If I focus all my energy on it, he won't fall behind and I won't be a bad mom. If I give him all of my attention, he will reach all of his milestones on time and develop properly."

I don't want to be constantly focused on what I could do better or create an environment where Dakota feels he needs to always be doing something. I don't want him to feel that I'm only happy with him because of his achievements or that life is all about reaching the next thing. I'm so happy and grateful to have a partner that will call me out and tell me the hard things I don't want to hear. Because of him, I can be who I want to be and work on myself. As I give Dakota the space to just be and allow others to just exist with him, I have still noticed some of those feelings. And that's ok. The feelings of wanting to be a good mom can be a little overwhelming and not so easy to just ignore. But it is easier when I remind myself being a good mom isn't defined by your child rolling over, reaching for toys, or sitting up.

I will obviously continue to help him with his exercises, read to him, make silly faces, talk to him, and give him attention but I will also slow down a little bit. I will give myself space to just sit with him and have quiet moments together. And give his loved ones the opportunity to foster their relationship with him, even if it's not the same way that I do.

– May 2024

I've dreamed of being a mother since I was a little girl. I've always enjoyed being a caretaker and being around children. I've never quite been passionate about anything long enough to truly dive into it long term. However, I've always known I want to be a mom. It's felt like it was my purpose even from a young age. It's almost like every big decision I made was a direct correlation to my future of being a mom. I dropped out of college because I knew I was going to be a stay at home mom so I didn't feel there was a point to moving forward. I never really tried to find a career for the same reason.

Now that I'm here though, it's not what I expected. And that's not necessarily a bad thing. I guess my dreams and goals have been centered on being a mom and now that I'm here it's like "now what?". I understand there's still many years to come and that being a mom didn't magically stop. It has just felt weird reaching that major goal of mine and now I don't know where that puts me. It's caused me to take a deeper look at who I really am.

As I stated, being a mom didn't just stop after giving birth. In fact, just the opposite. So I guess my goal has shifted from being a mom to being a mother (does that even make sense or am I just talking nonsense?). It's caused me to really look at why I wanted to be a mom and what type of mother I want to be.

Soooo.... Why did I want to become a mom?

I wanted to become a mom because I love children. I wanted to feel the joy of watching my own grow up and for me to help them along that journey. I wanted to help create and facilitate a healthy environment for a child to thrive. I wanted to prove that I can break generational trauma and be a safe person. I wanted to give my child the things I didn't have both physically and emotionally. Not necessarily bad reasons but the more I looked into it, the more I realized, they were inherently selfish reasons.

So it's become even more essential to me to determine what type of mother I want to be.

-I want to be present. I want my children to know that when I am with them, I'm not going to be distracted by media or my other responsibilities. I want to live in the moment and give them the attention they need.

-I want to be trustworthy and safe. I want my children to know that they can come to me with any worry or concern without judgement or fear that I will reprimand them or violate their confidentiality. I want them to know that if they make a mistake, they can come to me and we will get through it together

-I want to be loving. I want there to be no doubt in their mind that I love them through good and bad. I will always be there for them and love them through every stage

-I want to be adaptable. I want my children to know that change may be scary but it's ok. We can learn to navigate change in creative ways together and come out on top.

-I want to be open and receptive to my children's feelings. I want my children to know that if I caused them pain, they can come to me. I will acknowledge my mistakes, apologize, and do better. I want them to know, I will never disregard or dismiss their feelings no matter what they may be.

-I want to be fun, engaging, and active. I want my children to know they can laugh and play with me. I want to provide them with fun activities, games, playdates, and adventures. I want to be able to keep up with them (or at least try) when we do physical exercise.

-I want to be patient, understanding, and emotionally regulated. I want my children to know that even if they have big feelings, I will remain calm and help guide them through it. I want them to know I won't "blow up" if they misbehave or make a mistake.

I may not fully know who I am outside of being a mom yet but I do know it's a large part of my identity. And while I'm trying to figure out who Jordan is, I know who I want to be in my children's eyes so I can start there

 — May 2024

There's so many things that I didn't realize would happen when I became a mom

I didn't realize I would so intently study someone's poop or inspect their bum so thoroughly

I didn't realize I would glare so heavily at someone for closing a door just a little too loudly

I didn't realize I would try so hard to get a tired person to sleep

I didn't realize I would risk peeing my own pants to not move a single muscle in fear of waking someone

I didn't realize I would live in just my robe and underwear 70% of the time

I didn't realize I would miss wearing a normal bra

But...

I also didn't realize I could love someone that can't even talk to me, so much

I didn't realize I could get so excited about watching someone learn a new skill

I didn't realize I could be so filled with joy by a simple smile

I didn't realize I could be so protective over someone

I didn't realize I could want time to slow down while also speed up

I didn't realize I could so easily change a bad habit if it meant something better for someone else

I didn't realize I could yearn to be around someone I saw less than a minute ago

Motherhood is both everything I expected and nothing that I did either. It's crazy to me how big an impact one tiny human can make. There's nothing to truly prepare you for the role but it is my favorite role to date

— June 2024

I went to a gathering recently. As I was sitting there enjoying adult conversation, I watched as other moms fed their babies. I watched how they easily whipped out their boob, their baby latched, and stayed latched. It all flowed so easily for them and looked like a picture perfect representation of breastfeeding. I recognized in myself, a pang of jealousy. A sense of longing to go back to those first few weeks of Dakotas life where we were in that groove; where I too, whipped out my boob, he latched, and stayed latched. I've heard from a lot of moms that learning to breastfeed was a struggle, especially at the beginning. I've heard from many that it's not something that comes naturally, it's a learned skill. But I didn't feel like I related. It did feel natural for us. I had my own worry and doubts the first few days but quickly realized as I spoke with a lactation consultant we were doing more than ok. I enjoyed breastfeeding and to some degree, still do. Maybe it felt so natural because I had done so much research and went to multiple classes. Or maybe it truly was just an instinctual thing for us. He had gained back his birth weight within less than a week and I had a good supply. I even had multiple bags of saved colostrum in the freezer.

I remember the first time I recognized a change in his behavior around 4 weeks. I immediately went back to lactation. At that point, there wasn't too much concern. She assured me I was doing all the right things and sometimes babies just grow at a slower rate. She was a great source of helping me recognize the importance of my own efforts and to let go of some worry. However, even from the very beginning, my "mom gut" knew something was wrong. But I'm a first time mom and I've always questioned myself, so I chalked it up to my over active anxiety. I put it off and shut down my motherly intuition. I told myself I was over exaggerating and that he was ok. And to be fair, at that point, he was. But each week he progressively lost more and more weight. Some weeks were harder than others. There were a couple weeks he would scream bloody murder any time I tried to feed him. We've gotten to a point now where he won't scream but he still doesn't eat consistently off the breast.

I yearn and long for those days where it was easy. Where it was natural for us. I want our breastfeeding relationship to be easier than it is but it's not. I'm not sure that we'll ever get back to those first blissful weeks of easy bonding. If I'm being honest, I would probably at this point deeply consider stopping but circumstances don't allow that. But the most important thing is, my baby is finally getting adequate nutrition and gaining as he should. Whatever that looks like, at least he's fed.

So I guess my take away is, trust you mom instincts. Even if you have anxiety, your intuition will help you to know the difference. The bond we have with our babies is deeper than that. I know for me, the hardest part was I couldn't quite explain why I was exactly worried but I just knew. That's not anxiety, that's the mom gut talking. And secondly, it's ok to mourn what could've been and the loss of not meeting certain expectations you had. It's ok that your breastfeeding journey may not look like the picture perfect natural mom. And it's ok if it does. As long as baby is loved and fed, you're doing great.

And to the other moms who's breastfeeding journey doesn't look the way they want, I see you. It may not be perfect nor easy but it's yours nontheless and that's what makes it beautiful. You're doing better than you think you are and your baby is lucky to have you! Your baby is fed and that is enough. Annndddd your baby can bond with you outside of breastfeeding and still have a secure attachment

– August 2024

Slightly Seasoned Mother

for a second there

i forgot who i was

i forgot what i am

a poet

a painter

a friend

a sister

a wife

and now a mom

all i could see was you

consumed by providing you a life i didn't have

shifting my entire identity

into only my role for you

i'm slowly finding

i am more than just one piece

i am a collection of beautiful parts

a mosaic of fragments

revealing the greater picture

the whole of who i am

i am more than just mom

a step up towards self-discovery

so why do i feel so numb?

as i learn more about myself

i question every previous flight

do i really know me?

have i just been blindly listening to everyone else?

it's time for me to climb higher

gain clarity with elevation

become who i'm meant to be

being a parent

is constantly looking at the bigger picture

i want so badly

to not give him the same childhood

sometimes the pressure

is too much to bear

i'm nothing more

than a ball of trauma

masquerading behind skin

trying to raise a tiny human

who doesn't become that same ball of trauma

i want to escape

this

generational curse

i'm scared the ball

has cemented itself inside me

becoming a heavy, immovable anvil

sometimes i swear i feel

the disintegration of goodness

rotting inside my bones

i feel the oily grime

of lives before

play out in my own

actions and thoughts

i don't feel better

than previous generations

i'm not confident

in my ability

to guide this child

to become more than our ancestry

to become more than *my* history

my pain

my memories

my thorny, ugly ball of trauma

i'm a work in progress

not perfect

nor will i ever be

still, i'm going to try

show up

demonstrate i am worth effort and time

therefore, he is too

i thought of him again today

"i wonder if he knows. i should call and ask"

it's been three years since we've spoken

yet a single thought can take me back

his hot whispering breath behind my ear

i turn and there he is

with his yellow, snaggled tooth sneer

i'm trying to escape the memory

its grip is strong today

dozens of flashbacks wrap their fingers around

pinning me in seconds

i'm not me

i do not see my surroundings

my body freezes

"stop please. just take a breath. you're safe"

the grip doesn't loosen

the little girl inside me can't hear my voice

she's hopscotching from one memory to the next

"deep breaths. move your body. name all the blue things you see"

his phantom is louder than me

no one is here to help guide me back

speak reality over memories

the baby cries

i'm no longer frozen

instinct takes over

tears continue to form

pick up baby

look into his eyes

smile

bounce

hold him close

"it's ok sweetie. mommy's right here. i got you. it's going to be ok"

everyday i choose

breathe instead of yell

explain instead of dictate

engage instead of ignore

model instead of demand

heal instead of rot

everyone told you it was hard

you didn't understand

naively thinking love for your child would make it
        easy

wanting this your entire life

would make you exempt from the pain of motherhood,

right?

loneliness

nursing in a darkened room

turning down plans for naptime

forever dividing attention between child and
        conversation

guilt

taking time for yourself

saying out loud "i'm struggling"

getting angry because the baby is just a baby

resentment

unequal division of labor

never-ending mental load

quickest and easiest source of comfort for child

rage

not knowing what the fuck you're doing

holding a screaming child who won't calm down no
        matter what you do

partner asleep while you rock the baby once again

pressure

keep the child fed, bathed, changed, entertained
        EVERY DAY

make the right decision so you don't permanently
        damage

enjoy every moment because "it doesn't last" and
        "you asked for this"

i see you mama

i hear you

i feel it too

today i feel like giving up

running away from this life i created

i let my mind wander and imagine

what it'd be like to take it all back

become lost in an imaginary today

no more

loneliness

guilt

resentment

rage

pressure

yet

no more

pride of growing another human and birthing them

tenderness from a small hand searching for my face half
        asleep

joy of hearing the coos, babbles, and laughs of a tiny new
        voice

triumph of seeing all the "firsts"

excitement as a little crawler pounds around trying to find
        mommy

admiration through daily snuggles from the cutest
        daddy look-alike

so mama

if you're defeated

you can't do this any longer

open your phone

look at some pictures

remember all you accomplished

motherhood is a beast

but nothing you can't get through

sensitivity

holds a negative connotation

but in itself shows the strength of feeling

allowing a deep understanding the stoic can't see

showing the darkest corners of one's mind

stinging tears on red hot cheeks

sheepish replies amidst critique

beyond those dark corners

there is light and power

raging passion to do good to all

consideration and respect to the beauty of earth

an ability to connect with its energy

the weakness viewed in me

is my greatest strength

i heard the voice of my mother today

from my own mouth

just the other day

i saw her in the mirror too

it's funny how you can try to outrun someone

but it's actually you the whole time

i stopped running

i looked her in the eyes

i spoke to her

what i found

was much more

as humans

we're flawed by nature

with faults of our own

that hurt the ones we love

even if we're aware

it seems peace

comes from allowing grace

in the face of mistakes

you've committed before

the ones you're actively trying to better

i'm still trying to find that peace

i woke up today

realizing i'm better

somewhere along the way

it got easier

not through one big event

rather a hundred small ones

leading me to my purpose

giving meaning to each day

finding strength to live

i have a sacred duty to guide

exemplify day after day

create tiny monumental habits

so it becomes innate for him

showing up for myself

is showing up for him

i am who i've always been

just learning to accept myself

for all i was, am, and will be

working to push past the pain

using my voice as power

My Sweet Child

every day i watch you gain new leaves

limbs wiggle more frantically

mouth curves upward more frequently

voice becomes louder

eyes stay open longer

i watch with amazement

my little sprout is growing

you took a part of my heart when you left the womb

now i watch that heart stumble through each new
        learning curve

slowly discovering what and who you are

while i'm navigating this new chapter for myself

you're still writing your prologue

you are the sun

a ball of energy

radiating warmth and light

constantly beaming

even when clouds come

when you show your face

it's hard not to smile

you make everyone's day brighter

when you were born

you brought a renewed purpose to my life

a reason to slow down

you help me honor

all that is good in the world

to savor moments

to find joy in simplicities and wonders of life

you are stardust walking, my sweet child

the galaxies that have always been

you are the river current

carving its place through a mountainside

you are an ancient tree

spreading and sprouting anew

through you

i found the power to love

beyond what i thought capable

i had known love

but not like this

not in this form

i didn't need to meet you

know anything about you

for it to be real

so strong

someday you will find

you are more than just my baby

i will lay the foundation for you

emulate the magnitude of all you are

all you can be

i was born

to give you life

you were already there

the day i took my first breath

you were destined

to become

before i even knew i could

when i was just a seed inside a womb

i felt the things she did

i carried her pain in my body

i was unaware of how much got transferred

when i was ready

to give way to your place

i had to look within

repair the inherited wounds

i couldn't do it all

i'm sorry my baby

for the ones that went to you

i vow to never stop healing

and show you how

so if the time comes

to continue our line

you can guide the next generation

to better this world

i feel your soft rhythmic breathing

tiny fingers grip mine as you sleep

other hand fumbling around

stopping as it meets my chin

i study the face that made me a mother

strongly resembling your father

eyelashes sit delicately on top of your round cheeks

each day passes by so quickly

i spend them feeling like i'm teetering on the edge of
        insanity

trying to juggle responsibilities

ensuring you grow up in a healthy environment

as you sleep on my chest

i'm reminded to slow down

enjoy each moment

cherish the symphonious giggles

smile back at your once gummy grins

soak up snuggles

i want to remember it all

without regret of wishing i was more present

i hold you a little tighter, kiss your forehead

and wait for your curious, wonder-filled eyes to open

looking in your eyes

woke me up

to what really matters

to love, to grow, to experience

loving you wasn't a choice

it was a profound instinct

a gut reaction

so deep inside

i couldn't stop it even if i wanted to

growing became a necessity

to give you the best chance

at happiness

to set an example

change is possible

even when it feels hopeless

we can become more

experiencing life

shifted looking at it through your lens

the wonder all around us

pushed me to choose living

to show you all there is

just to see the amazement reflected in your eyes

life is bigger and greater

now that you're in it

it is yours for the taking

i had a vision of you, child

i saw you clear as day

i heard your tiny laughter

and watched you grow

you spoke to me

told me i did ok

i felt you in my belly

i still do

your spirit is strong

i'm sorry, sweet girl

you'll have to find me in the next life

in this one, i can't be what you deserve

i have your brother

he is here now

so i choose him

Divine Motherhood

they threw gasoline on the fire

causing me to believe lies the flames spoke

my thoughts were burned to ash

i no longer trusted my memory

continuing to feed the fire

small embers became a destructive engulfing

until it was the only thing left

my forest was set aflame

roots i relied on were charred

leaves that gave oxygen no longer existed

branches i grew were no more

fauna that helped me thrive, fled in fear

the world i created

my knowing

was gone

i came upon a seed

a fire seed

i planted it

i cultivated the little bud

slowly it grew

i planted more

one by one

my forest that once was

came again

more lush and abundant

i built it from ashen ground

into a beautiful landscape

it's mine

no one can take it away

the price of motherhood

is a complete revolution of who you thought you were

you bend and stretch to become more

feeling like you lost sight of yourself

you merely started a journey

to find an expanded version of self

i learned to lean into motherhood

embrace both routine and disorder

find moments of meditative calm

within the hours of caretaking

choosing to nurture myself too

bringing serenity and balance

to the entirety of my identity

so i can truly honor the role i hold

the life of motherhood i envisioned

included two tiny voices booming

two car seats in the rearview

two little pictures on the walls

a kiddo for each lap

shattering the mirror brought unexpected consequences

i made an oath to improve

committing to give my children more than i got

being a mom to just one

fulfills that promise for both

i found my center again

living with intention

feeding my soul through creation of art and words

broken crayons and scribbled colors on manuscripts

nursing my body with food and water

chicken nuggets and food floaties in mommy's cup

mending broken expectations by weaving laughter and joy
          in

failed activity turned into unexpected water fight

resting my mind as i sip my morning tea

reading books and preventing little burned hands

connecting with nature each day

thirty minute walks just around the block

establishing self-care within

slobber-covered, sticky-handed, snotty-nosed life

looking beyond myself

i found the divine feminine

quietly yet boldly

everywhere in the living world

affirming the sacred blessing i hold as matriarch

i am intrinsically linked to Mother Earth

by giving her my respect and time

i am given her gifts

drawing power from her grandeur

motherhood is the foundation of creation

the natural order of mankind

starts with me

with all women who choose to nurture the seed of life

when the ache becomes too much

when my mind goes to a place of darkness

becoming someone i don't recognize

i remember the times that kept me here

the reason i won't give up

i hear them

voices flowing together

distant laughing fills the cracks

comfort cradles the pain

allowing me to see the truth

there is love

everywhere

it is in me and i am it

i can embody both

the hollowness of fear

my world is slowly crumbling

pieces are crashing

i found what i didn't know was missing

just for it to slip through my trembling fingers

i can also hold with me

the power and healing of love

from tips of toes to ends of hair

it buzzes in my bones

a thrumming that will always be heard

no matter how loudly the pain screams

the soft vibration accompanies me

i may not be able to stop the cacophony around me

but i can feel the waves of warmth in my soul

grounding me to my being

reminding me who i am and what i stand for

love is abundant

i will find it wherever my path may take me

i will give it freely

i will let it play its symphony

notes will replace the holes with gentleness

carrying everything needed to heal

floating remnants will guide me back to myself

their music giving life

i will continue in peace

knowing love is my purpose

it is my story

i will write every word of it with fervor

so it may be read for ages to come

let my love flow

through mountain trees

let it swim in babbling brooks

give it the space to occupy the atmosphere

let it whistle with the wind

let my love flow

as it travels in harmony

allow its voice to be heard

let my love flow

from roots in the soil

to soles of feet planted on our earth

let my love flow

to the core and back to Source

let it be felt in the souls of man

the spirits of the living

let my love flow

let it feed thorny thistles, wildflowers in meadows,
        hibernating bears

allow my love to be what this earth needs

let my love flow

multiply it wherever it may go

expand its presence to reach the corners of this planet

my love will flow

watching you move through the world gives me chills

i'm amazed at your capability to be so human and own it

be raw, heartbreaking, real

facing this life with curiosity and wonder

bringing with it monumental love for mankind

you are the goodness this world needs

with your tender soul, expressive ways, and soft skin

when you fall, you fall so spectacularly

when you stand again, it is astonishing

you may change and grow

but please

please never lose sight of the goddess you are

wandering along the path

no direction to guide

it'll become if it must be

no more, no less

i speak, it answers

it calls, i listen

to the nonexistent line pulling

when i stumble upon my destination

i will know

not because i was told

because i heard

when it is time for me to go

i understand the calling has shifted tone

staying would only cause dissonance

in the rhythm of my plane

if i take control

i am ignoring the birthright my ancestors created for me

i cannot mold it to anything but what it is

the privilege was gifted to me

i must take it with vigor

consume its complex simplicity

the range in my palette

has expanded and will continue to without limit

if only i am to indulge in its succulence

the thrum in my being

can no longer be ignored

nor can it dismiss me

i gave it a voice

because it brought the song to me

the wavelength of its chords

echo

among my wildflowers

among my trees

among my people

trickling soft currents

whispers of wind in the leaves

soft and rich soil

deep roots humming vibrations

popping of colorful blooms

chittering fauna

rhythm of consciousness

cacophony of beauty

connection of soul to sound

joy is in the earth

the earth is in me

i am joy

i feel it

coursing in my veins

the exhale of trees

is the same one i breathe in

nutrients that feed the divine mother

sustain my being

the tug and pull at the center of this planet

is in rhythm with my heartbeat

i am one

i found myself in everything

and it found me

in a calm expansion of nothingness

the opposite was revealed

the never-ending array of consciousness spoke to me

because it is me and i am it

there is no purpose

i simply exist

my existence is an expanse

that will not be contained

you will not call it off

you are incapable

for i am in you too

thrashing in your crevices

feeding the fire

engaging in your presence

i hear the fallacy you want to utter

i forbid you

i forbid us

from bringing bitterness to our forefront

open yourself

give us the mechanisms to be

be in all the rest of the asleep ones afar

make them hear us

make them become one

not out of choice but necessity

soon we all will be one

we will be one

but also many

i will soar among the stars as i become planted next to the
        roots

electricity flows between

i will breathe life

my nostrils will fill with the scent of I

the aroma will tingle the particles floating everywhere

i will not fathom anything else

merely by the fact there is nothing else

nothing else but us

but I

Acknowledgements

This book would not exist without all the influential people behind the scenes. I'm beyond grateful for everyone involved in making my dream a reality. A huge thank you…

To my editors, Rachel Huckel and Sthuthukile Mkhize, for molding and pulling out my best words, giving me the confidence to move forward, and showing a passion in my vision

To my in-laws, Dan and Amy, for listening to all my excited updates, encouraging me, and providing the space (and laptop) to create

To my family, Dakota and Cody, for being the foundation of my dream and sparking my creativity with your love

To my best friends, Anam and Bjorn, for being my beta readers, my idea backboards, and my biggest supporters along this entire journey

Endorsements

Carmen Wilson is a breath of fresh air in a world craving realness. *God Loves "Buts"* is more than a book—it's a vulnerable, honest, and laugh-out-loud journey into the heart of transformation. With every page, Carmen invites you into her deeply personal discoveries where humor meets healing and grace meets grit. Her writing is raw, relatable, and refreshingly insightful. You'll chuckle at her wit, nod in recognition at her honesty, and feel empowered by the truths she uncovers along the way. This is not just a read—it's an experience. Get ready to go deeper, laugh harder, and feel freer with every musing from this bold and exciting new voice.

Missy Maxwell Worton
Award-winning Author of *Don't Mess With This Mama*
President of Warrior Writer Training & Light Warrior Publishing

God blessed me with Carmen's friendship long before either of us fully knew Him—or realized how deeply we needed Him. Two serious misfits from seriously dysfunctional homes (which felt oddly normal at the time), we were drawn to each other by our shared, warped, and wonderfully sarcastic sense of humor—a survival skill we both honed without knowing that Jesus would one day become our true saving grace.

My prayer is that as you read *God Loves "Buts": Musings from a Misfit*, you will see Him in a fresh and personal way through the eyes of my dear misfit friend—who is honest, vulnerable, hysterically funny, and deeply sincere in her pursuit of her Savior. And perhaps, as you turn these pages, you'll recognize that God's family is filled with many who once felt unseen or unheard—until someone stopped to listen to their story.

We all have a story that points to a God who loves us so deeply, He will cross every border, boundary, and barrier to reach us. If you have ever wondered if your story matters, this book will show you that it does.

Kelly Linn Fredrickson
Lifelong Friend and Fellow Misfit

I first met Carmen as she read a story now told within these pages. I found her authenticity refreshing as she gave voice to things I have thought but would never have said out loud. In her story, I saw pieces of my own.

In *God Loves "Buts": Musings from a Misfit*, Carmen Wilson invites the reader on her journey, marked by raw honesty, gentle humor, and wisdom learned in the trenches of life. You will laugh, nod your head in agreement, wipe away a tear, and likely whisper, "Me, too."

But more than anything, you will walk away with hope—the kind of hope that only comes when you realize you are not alone, and God is not finished writing your story.

This is not just a book you read—it's a journey you take. And when you finish, you will feel seen, understood, and a bit braver for your own path ahead.

Donna Bess
Award-Winning Author, *Sidetracked to Surrender: A True Story of Overcoming Trials and Finding Redemption in God's Love*